The Beginner's Guide to Starting a Small Business

Learn to think like an entrepreneur, sell your product profitably, successfully market it, & much more!

Victoria Sharp

© Copyright 2022 - All rights reserved.

The content contained within this book may not be reproduced, duplicated, or transmitted without direct written permission from the author or the publisher.

Under no circumstances will any blame or legal responsibility be held against the publisher, or author, for any damages, reparation, or monetary loss due to the information contained within this book. Either directly or indirectly. You are responsible for your own choices, actions, and results.

Legal Notice:

This book is copyright protected. This book is only for personal use. You cannot amend, distribute, sell, use, quote, or paraphrase any part, or the content within this book, without the consent of the author or publisher.

Disclaimer Notice:

Please note the information contained within this document is for educational and entertainment purposes only. All effort has been executed to present accurate, up-to-date, reliable, complete information. No warranties of any kind are declared or implied. Readers acknowledge that the author is not engaging in the rendering of legal, financial, medical, or professional advice. The content within this book has been derived from various sources. Please consult a licensed professional before attempting any techniques outlined in this book.

By reading this document, the reader agrees that under no circumstances is the author responsible for any losses, direct or indirect, which are incurred as a result of the use of the information contained within this document, including, but not limited to, — errors, omissions, or inaccuracies.

Your Free Gift

As a way of saying thanks for your purchase, I'm offering my readers TWO Ultimate Mini Guides for FREE.

To get instant access, just scan this QR Code:

Inside these books, you will discover:
- The essentials to starting a new business
- What is project management, and where to begin
- And so much more!

Grab these free books if you want to start taking immediate action on your business.

TABLE OF CONTENTS

Introduction 4

Thinking Like an Entrepreneur 7

What Are You Selling? 12

Your Value Proposition 18

What Is Your Business Model? 26

Do You Need a Business Plan? 31

Handling Your Finances 37

Marketing And Promotions 44

Conclusion 50

SNEAK PEAK: THE PLAYBOOK FOR STARTING A SMALL BUSINESS 52

Resources 66

Introduction

"Success is not final; failure is not fatal: it is the courage to continue that counts." – *Winston Churchill*

According to CB Insights, a poor business model causes about 19% of new enterprises to fail yearly. Launching a business can be an incredibly intriguing pursuit; as such, everyone who attempts to go down this path hopes they will succeed. However, many people who launch firms or businesses end up closing their doors after some time. According to research data, numerous enterprises are started each month, and a substantial percentage fail. What causes the failures, and why? It's simple; they lacked a solid foundation before getting started.

Over the years, I have been opportune to serve on the board of several small businesses. I learned a lot from them, even though some didn't succeed in the end. One specific concept, however, stands out in my assessment of failed businesses: they have a fundamentally weak foundation. People tend to enter the business world without first doing their homework, with no business plan and uncertainty about what exactly they should be selling. This is a recipe for failure.

To be clear, business ownership is a difficult task. More new businesses fail than succeed, but this book was written to prevent your business from being part of that statistic. I have created this guide using the combined experiences of various entrepreneurs with extensive business knowledge.

I aim to leverage this publication by sharing many of my hard-learned lessons, seeking to help individuals considering starting an enterprise and ensuring they receive all the necessary information to scale their business successfully.

In this handy book, you're going to learn…

- What a successful entrepreneur thinks about
- How to know what you should sell
- Your tailored value propositions
- What a business model is
- How to handle your finances intelligently
- How to market and promote your business

This book will detail all the knowledge you need to succeed as an entrepreneur. With that knowledge, you will be able to manage your company efficiently. Please keep an open mind as you begin reading and take notes as you go!

Chapter 1

Thinking Like an Entrepreneur

"The successful warrior is the average man, with laser-like focus." – Bruce Lee

An entrepreneurial mindset, by definition, is how you think about and approach the world around you from a business standpoint. It also has a lot to do with the type of person you are, your skills, and your approach to life in general. An entrepreneurial mindset can be developed over time, but it's not innate and does not materialize without effort. This chapter will discuss the qualities you should imbibe to be a successful entrepreneur with a mindset to match.

The first step to building an entrepreneurial mindset is understanding what an entrepreneur does. Entrepreneurship is a process, not an individual action. Entrepreneurship is about solving problems through creative thinking and quick decision-making. Entrepreneurs are problem solvers who see opportunities where others see only obstacles; they can see the invisible forces in play around them and act on those unseen forces with confidence and conviction.

Entrepreneurship is a lot like changing the world. When

you become an entrepreneur, you alter how things happen in your specific industry. You are moving from being a consumer to being a creator. You are taking something that already exists and changing it into something fresh and improved. As an entrepreneur, you may wield power to change your industry in any number of ways: by changing prices, offering new services or products that people want, changing attitudes or perceptions, opening up entirely new markets where none existed before, or even by creating completely new products that nobody has ever thought of before.

The best entrepreneurs think like creators because they understand their ideas' power. They recognize that what they have is more valuable than any other business idea — and they take advantage of this fact daily. A powerful entrepreneurial mindset is the ability to see your business as a unique opportunity, not just another job or pipe dream. Entrepreneurship is about being proactive in your business, not reactive. It's about anticipating problems and solving them before they become crises. Great entrepreneurs constantly ask themselves: "What can I do?" and "What problem should I be solving?" They realize that every action has an equal and opposite reaction. Entrepreneurs solve problems by creating more opportunities for themselves and their customers—not by reacting to what others are doing.

Characteristics of Great Entrepreneurs

Entrepreneurial success isn't solely dependent on your idea or your resources alone. Many individuals have great ideas and a lot of money to spend, yet they never quite manage to be successful in their endeavors. Look inwardly and consider whether or not you possess the following traits when considering if you truly want to become an entrepreneur. And remember, you can always work to acquire these qualities later on to increase your chances of success.

- Acceptance of risk

Entrepreneurs develop their ability to weigh and evaluate risk and how it aligns with their comfort level by committing time and money to unproven businesses and concepts.

- Innovation and creativity

Creative problem solvers are often also entrepreneurs. To solve pressing problems, they use novel tools and strategies.

- Future orientation

Entrepreneurs consider the future and assume responsibility for all results. They may be motivated by success and achieving objectives for themselves or their ideas.

- Adaptability and flexibility

Entrepreneurs not only adapt to change but also anticipate it. They anticipate challenges, setbacks, and new knowledge and are quick to respond to them.

- Initiative and independence

Entrepreneurs have the drive to succeed and are self-starters. As a result, they are naturally ready to take on any difficulties head-on rather than to look for advice or direction.

To be an entrepreneur, you must first think like one. Some say you should "think like a startup," but that's not necessarily true. You can only imagine how startups operate if you've been inside one, and you can't launch a startup unless you're in love with the idea of starting it. If you're not in love with it, then don't do it. Why would anyone care if you aren't fully invested in the idea?

So, how do you fall in love with the idea of starting something new? Three things make entrepreneurs experience this passion:

1) They have a burning desire to fix a problem;

2) They believe that there is a market for their solution; and

3) They have confidence they can build something better than what currently exists.

You don't need all three things at once. Suppose you don't care about fixing a problem or building something better than what currently exists. In that case, there's no point in starting a company because your customers won't be excited about your product or services anyway. But, if you have all three things in place, you'll have the chance to be an entrepreneur — even after your company becomes successful!

Key Takeaways

- An entrepreneurial mindset can be developed over time but is not innate or born from nothing.

- Entrepreneurial success isn't solely dependent on your idea or your resources.

Do you know precisely what you want to offer? If you do, is it the right thing for you? Having an entrepreneurial mindset is just one small step in the right direction. The next chapter will discuss everything you need to know about selling the right product.

Chapter 2

What Are You Selling?

"Make something people want and sell that, or be someone people need and sell you."

— Ryan Lilly

A big question many intending entrepreneurs fail to ask. It would help if you understood the distinctiveness between what you want to sell and what people want to buy. That understanding is key to defining your success as a business owner. When you understand that, you won't just start a business, you will first understand the need. The truth is, there is always a need that might differ from what you think. Without finding out what that is, you won't be able to meet customers' expectations.

One of the most prevalent misconceptions when starting a small business is that you will always produce and sell products that people want. The truth is: that in almost every industry, a need exists. It may be wiser to address these needs than specific consumer desires. You'll be able to start by thinking about what you are selling as a potential small business owner. Are you in a niche or a service industry? Do you have something people need and an inherent desire to purchase?

In this chapter, you will learn what to sell, why to sell your products, and how to position your sales strategy to get the right customers. The first step in starting a business is figuring out what you will sell in the first place. I'd like to think there's no secret formula for making money, but there are ways that people succeed and fail when it comes to creating that "next big thing."

Have Something People Want

You're selling your product or service. You might be selling a product (like a children's toy or electronic gadget), or you might be selling a service (like job counseling or wedding planning). Whatever the case, your product or service is ultimately what you're offering buyers. Knowing what people want before seeking consumers is crucial in making intelligent business decisions. Unfortunately, this concept is also why it's so challenging to start a business and make sales right out of the gate: you won't know what people want until they find out for themselves!

Write out these questions, and think of an answer for each of them; if you're unable to do so, you may want to wait before kickstarting a business:

- What is your product or service? Is it an app? Real estate? A cookbook? A software program?

- What is the problem you are trying to solve for your customers?

- How do you differentiate yourself from the competition and make a compelling offer to clients?

- Who is your ideal client? Why do they need to buy from you?

Be Someone People Need

Your target market isn't going to buy from you if they don't need what you're selling. So, how do you figure out who needs what?

By researching your specific market, of course!

What marketable skills, expertise, or experience do you have?

Almost everyone has at least some knowledge or skills that have the potential to be profitable. For instance, the origin of Snap-On Tools can be traced back to two machinists, Joe Johnson and William Seidemann. They created a set of interchangeable sockets and wrench handles to facilitate their work. Because Johnson and Seidemann were seasoned machinists and thought their idea was excellent, they continued to develop it after their employer flatly rejected it. Another instance is how fast-food manager R. David Thomas used his knowledge to launch Wendy's burger company (named after his daughter) after helping Colonel Sanders thrive with his Kentucky Fried Chicken franchise.

Do my ideas have to be brand new?

It's not necessary to have the most cutting-edge business concepts. An old idea can occasionally be used for inspiration and presented in a new market with astounding results. Leopoldo Pujals, for instance, established TelePizza in 1987 after seeing Domino's Pizza's speedy home delivery during his travels through the United States. The business had launched 1,025 locations worldwide by 2010 and completed an IPO in April 2016 for about €550 million. So, your ideas don't have to be brand new; they could be based on an existing passion for something or your hobbies, which could convert into a helpful service to your target audience.

Improve your communication abilities.

You must be excellent at verbal and nonverbal communication, which is just as important as comprehending your consumers' characteristics and demands. A competent seller must possess soft skills, emotional intelligence, and exceptional communication abilities. Unless they are the only seller of the goods and you genuinely need it to survive, you won't buy anything from someone who cannot communicate effectively.

Don't be afraid to ask for help from experts or admit your own mistakes.

Rather than asking for advice, ask for your family, friends, or potential customers frank feedback, more details, or data, which can tell a whole different story. Then, find someone who can provide you with new insight into a situation you may not have thought of.

Everyone, regardless of identity, requires assistance in life. Knowing who to turn to for help and conducting a thorough initial investigation is crucial. Once that is finished, talk to the expert and explain your issue before sharing what you learned from your research. This will demonstrate to them that you require their knowledge.

Key Takeaways

- Find out how to serve people and get busy satisfying that need with a product or service.
- Build a solid foundation for your business idea with the questions asked in this chapter.

- Be honest and respectful with everyone you do business with. This includes customers, suppliers, employees, etc.

- You can be successful if you have ethical business practices and a good product.

Right now, I'm selling the ability to make people in your communities happy. This is a business book, but it's also my life philosophy and summarizes why I started my business. I believe that if you can help people in any way, you should do it. If you can inspire them, make them laugh, and be more confident along the way, then do it. The most important thing is to have something of value people want because if you don't have something people want, then nobody will buy it from you. This leads us to Chapter Three, where we will discuss the Value Proposition.

Chapter 3

Your Value Proposition

"The foundation of any strategy implementation is consistent alignment of internal capabilities and processes with the customer value proposition." — Robert S. Kaplan

A value proposition is a declaration of the benefits a customer can expect to receive from your business. It's the main reason a potential customer should work with you. Additionally, it is the most prominent factor in determining whether visitors will stick around to learn more about your goods or click the "back" button on your website. Therefore, your value proposition is the major component of your website that needs testing; if done well, it will significantly increase traffic.

In fact, "test your value proposition" would be my one piece of conversion optimization advice. The stronger your value proposition, the more well-known your firm will be. The absence of a value proposition was one of the most prevalent flaws I saw when I assessed many websites in my primary market. Admittedly, it can be challenging to define your value proposition. There could be five or six excellent reasons for clients to spend money on your services in some circumstances.

It may not always be simple to distinguish your good or service from your rivals.

This chapter will delve into defining your value proposition, the elements of a good one, and how to put it to work. First, it's worthwhile to search thoroughly for your value proposition. Then, when you know what your customers genuinely value, you can highlight that in your marketing and advertising campaigns to increase sales. Your value proposition is not a positioning statement, tagline, or catchphrase. Your value proposition can be used to determine these things, but that does not mean they are the same.

Formulating Your Value Proposition

Your value proposition should address the following inquiries:

- What goods or services do you offer?
- What value or ultimate advantage does your product offer?
- Who is your ideal client?
- What distinguishes your goods or services from those of your rivals?

A value proposition, in essence, is a concise statement that provides three things: a one-sentence headline and a two to three-sentence paragraph outlining what you offer, who it's for, and why it's helpful is a solid format to follow. You can also include images of your product, a hero shot, a list of essential features or benefits, and a description.

Relevancy. Describe how your product helps clients and improves their lives.

Measured worth. We are communicating particular advantages.

Differentiation. Explain to your ideal client why they should buy from you rather than your rivals.

A value proposition is something that everyday people should be able to comprehend easily. It is intended for readers and consumers. Here is an illustration of what a value proposition should not look like:

"Revenue-focused marketing automation & sales effectiveness tools unleash teamwork."

If you need a little extra inspiration, there are several other examples when you look this term up online.

Analyze your service or product

Think about the issues or hurdles your clients may face and how you intend to resolve them. Then, consider the psychological and practical needs you are attempting to meet. If you work as a financial advisor, you might not only purchase stocks and bonds for your clients. It would help if you also gave them specialized financial advice, so they know their money is safe and used wisely. In addition, you may establish your value proposition by focusing on how you make your client's lives simpler and more enjoyable.

Direct access to the source

Not sure what your customers appreciate about your company? Please don't hesitate to question them; nobody knows better than they do why they prefer to purchase from you. In exchange for a small gift, coupon code, or entry into a drawing, ask them to respond to a brief survey on why they decided to work with you instead of your competitors. Ask respondents in your survey what motivated them to make a purchase.

Is it of high caliber?

A distinctive choice?

An excellent place to be?

A welcoming staff?

Low costs?

You may be surprised by their responses. You may also try conducting a quick customer survey if you have a sizable email marketing list to learn what motivated them to purchase from you in the first place.

For this example, let's discuss a startup gym that offers memberships.

(Note: I encourage you to create examples that relate to your business niche to understand the concept fully.)

Describe the issue being resolved

Some individuals enjoy going to the gym. So, B-King Fitness has established a welcoming environment and offers membership options at reasonable prices for anyone who may be wary of the gym or finds it frightening and pricey. But working out as you are and not worrying about fitting into the stereotype of the typical gym goer is the key perk.

Another illustration could be for a startup marketing agency. A powerful value proposition would be: making it simple for small businesses with tight budgets to sell their goods and services. With so many options for business marketing these days, our services help our clients decide how to allocate their marketing budgets. We make a real effort to gain our clients' trust and become true partners. We handle the minutiae, giving them up to manage their expanding business, which is what they do best.

A generic value proposition will produce uninspiring outcomes. On the other hand, your value proposition will be more persuasive the more explicit and detailed you can be. Seek to thoroughly explain why your target audience should choose you over the competition to solve their problem.

Test your marketing efforts

It is time to refine your value proposition even further once you have reduced the field of prospective value propositions to two or three candidates. Test email subject lines highlighting specific value propositions you consider if you have an email newsletter. Keep an eye on their open rates (and Certified Therapeutic Recreation Specialists (CTRs) to determine the most effective ones.

Don't only test your value proposition with words. See how your customers react by posting photographs on social media that highlight your value offer.

Avoid using hype language or corporate jargon

One mistake you must be careful of is using hype words or business jargon in writing your value proposition. Not only is it unprofessional to have it that way, but it is also written most times in your language instead of your customers'. That way, it would be able to meet the conversation that is already going through consumers' minds. Remember, what you say about your products differs from how customers describe them.

Avoid bland Ads

Don't create an uninteresting value proposition. It will quickly turn your prospects off and make you lose patronage. Bland ads lack solid and convincing features that can attract customers. So, no magic can help you command sales if you have one. When your clients discover your ads are not compelling enough, they will have zero concern for anything you are advertising. It is that simple.

Explain how you are superior to the competition

The gyms that put a strong emphasis on pushing their clients to their limits are those that compete with B-King Fitness. There are no requirements to complete reps or circuits or to achieve an absurdly low body fat percentage at B-King Fitness. Instead, they advertise their facility as a non-gym replacement for the standard health club, widening their intended demographic.

Key Takeaways

- The general public should be able to read and comprehend your value offer.

- Ensure your value proposition conveys the advantages a customer will experience using your product or service.

- Avoid using hype language or corporate jargon.

- Always avoid bland advertising.

You'll be able to see if you're concentrating on the right value proposition within three to six months. If you feel you are not working with the most beneficial proposition, go back to the drawing board and test out your other candidates. Finding your value proposition can be challenging, but the effort will be worthwhile once you do.

It is time to establish a sound business structure to go along with your impactful value proposition, which will be covered in more detail in the following chapter. Comprehensive business structures aid young, developing businesses in luring capital, hiring talent, and inspiring management and personnel.

Chapter 4

What Is Your Business Model?

"Startups don't fail because they lack a product; they fail because they lack customers and a profitable business model." - Steve Blank

Imagine constructing a house without a blueprint in place. Funny, right? It's the same way establishing a business requires a business model. A business model is a blueprint for how a company will make money. It's how the company generates revenue and turns those revenues into profits. It's a blueprint for how you plan to sustain your business over time to grow into something bigger and more profitable later.

Business models are important because they help us gain more insight into whether or not a company will succeed. A great business model makes sense from a customer perspective. It should solve a problem that buyers have, deliver on their needs while also having some financial upside for them, and have enough flexibility that it can evolve as your business grows.

Types Of Business Model

Business to Business (B2B) is a business that sells its product or service to other businesses. One example is a manufacturer that sells their widgets to wholesalers, who sell them to retailers.

Business to Consumer (B2C) is a business that sells its product or service directly to consumers, usually generating direct income and building brand loyalty. Examples include restaurants and stores that sell food or clothes directly to customers and online companies like Amazon that sell products directly through their websites.

Subscription Bases form when customers pay for access to something regularly, such as software upgrades, web services, magazines, or email newsletters. Some brands offer services requiring customers to subscribe before they can enjoy them. So, access is given upon subscription. Examples of such brands include Netflix, Spotify, and Apple Music.

Steps To Creating a Profitable Business Model

State the problem you want to solve

The problem you want to solve can be a functional issue or an emotional one. Choose no more than three significant issues that your solution will address.

Pinpoint the primary client and the main issue

You must decide on one of the top three client types and one or more of the top three problems to concentrate your efforts on. This is because a business model can develop in various ways, and focusing on the path of action can improve the model's execution and experimentation. After this process, you will have one main client or critical problem to concentrate on.

Establish a range of potential solutions

List as many as ten possible solutions to the issue. Next, pick three from those ten that can be easily implemented and won't require much time or money to kickstart (this is a one-day business model). Then, choose one of these three to move forward with.

Establish a range of potential business models for the solution

You will have determined a product or service for your chosen solution and the customer type by this point. Next, describe five monetization techniques that could be used for that good or service. Keep at least two handy that can be tried right away.

Try, then decide

Test the product and the monetization plan to see which was most effective.

Business Model Example

Consider this example; Company A is into leasing and selling video games. After investing $3 million, the company got $6 million as a return. That means they were able to garner $ 3 million as gains. However, the following year, internet hitches occurred, and everything disrupted the market, but the company scaled through. The company leverages its business model to adapt to the changes without much difficulty. As a result, it recorded a higher increase in profit despite the interruption. That is one of the benefits of having a business model. It helps you salvage any unpleasant situation that may arise while running it.

When developing a business model, it is essential to *take your time*. You might have some ideas for names, prices, and perfect locations scribbled down on paper. Although that's a terrific start, developing a sound business plan takes time. Launching a small business is thrilling, but you must provide the best basis for its success. The value of your customers should not be estimated; instead, do your research. To determine the genuine worth of the solution your product or service gives to the market, poll your friends and tap into your professional network. Developing your business model slowly will prevent you from underestimating or overestimating anything.

Key Takeaways

- Business models are important because they help us to understand whether or not a company will be successful in the long run.

- A great business model makes sense from a customer perspective. It should solve a problem that buyers have and deliver on their needs while also having some financial upside for them.

What are your business plans now that you have identified your business model? Mapping out a business plan is essential because it gives your business the foundation you need to move forward. This is your direction, and without it, your business will drift in too many different directions at once. Having a foundational idea of what you want to achieve with your company can go a long way towards making that happen. The next chapter will outline business plans and how they can benefit your enterprise.

Chapter 5

Do You Need a Business Plan?

"Plan for what is difficult while it is easy, do what is great while it is small." – Sun Tzu

According to the most recent statistic, 32.5 million small firms make up 99.9% of all US businesses (SBA, 2021). In this chapter, we will discuss why it is crucial for these small businesses to have a business plan and the elements and strategies associated with drafting a business plan.

Understanding Business Plans

A business plan is a written document that describes a company's primary operations and how it plans to achieve its goals. Startup enterprises use business plans to gain traction and draw in outside investors. An executive team can utilize a business plan as an internal roadmap to maintain focus and progress toward short and long-term goals.

Elements of a Business Plan

- **Mission statement:** This statement is included in the executive summary, including crucial details about the company's management, personnel, operations, and location.

- **Products and services:** This section is where businesses can describe the goods and services they will provide. It may also communicate the processes used in production and manufacturing, the company's patents, and proprietary technology as other elements that may be considered. You can also add research and development information (R&D).

- **Market analysis:** A company must clearly grasp its target market and industry and conduct a comprehensive study to follow its business plan. Additionally, it will outline the anticipated consumer demand for a company's goods or services and how simple or challenging it may be to overtake market leaders.

- **Marketing strategy:** This section outlines the company's plans for reaching consumers and attracting and retaining a customer base. There needs to be a defined distribution channel.

- **Budget:** Every business must have an operating budget in place. Costs associated with hiring employees, product development, production, marketing, and any other business-related expenses should be listed in this area.

- **Monetary projections:** A set of financial forecasts for the company must be included in a thorough business plan. They consist of the company's marketing plan, the total budget, the market study, and the existing and future financial requirements.

- **Financial planning:** For established businesses, financial statements, balance sheets, and other financial data may be presented in this section. Potential investors and new firms' targets and estimations for the first few years will also be described.

How To Write a Business Plan

A well thought and well-written business plan can significantly benefit a firm. Although templates are available for company plans, avoid creating a generic document. A detailed summary, company description, market analysis, product or service description, marketing plan, financial predictions, and an appendix should be the first elements of the framework (for documents that support the main sections). Any requests you make for money may be part of your strategy. Your plan's main body should not exceed 20 to 25 pages.

Reasons to write a business plan

- To raise capital for your company.

Before they offer you money, potential lenders or investors want to see a detailed business plan. Unfortunately, a simple explanation of your business idea is insufficient. Instead, make sure you have a specific business and financial program that outlines your chances of success and the amount of funding you will require for long-term success.

- To make wise choices.

A business plan can help you, as an entrepreneur, clarify and concentrate on your business ideas and strategies. With a documented plan, you can more easily focus on management challenges, human resource planning, technology, and adding value for your customers in addition to financial matters.

- To assist you in determining any potential flaws.

A business strategy aids in pointing out potential hazards in your concept that you may have overlooked previously. After identifying these risks, you can include possible solutions to combat these issues in your business plan (to reference when they arise).

- To share your concepts with key stakeholders.

You can use a business plan as a communication tool to entice lenders or financial organizations to provide you with investment funds. Additionally, you can use it to persuade individuals to work for your company, obtain credit from suppliers, and draw in potential clients.

A lot of thought goes into writing a company plan. First, consider your goals and utilize them as a springboard for action. It does not have to be overly challenging or complicated. Your plan's primary components should outline where you are now, where you want your business to go, and how you will get there. Even though it cannot ensure success, a strong business strategy can significantly lower the likelihood of failure. Furthermore, without a plan to direct them, your entrepreneurial ideas would fail rapidly, even if you were not looking for financing.

Key Takeaways

- A business plan is a written document that describes a company's primary operations and how it plans to achieve its goals.

- A well thought and well-written business plan can significantly benefit a firm. Although templates are available for company plans, avoid creating a generic document.

- A business plan can help you, as an entrepreneur, clarify and concentrate on your business ideas and strategies.

For any prospective business owner, education on financial literacy is the most crucial stage of the process. Business owners can build a secure financial future and prevent failure by being familiar with the fundamental abilities required to operate a small business, such as doing essential accounting duties, asking for a loan, or producing financial statements. The next chapter will outline how you can intelligently handle your finances.

Chapter 6

Handling Your Finances

"Money wants to remain and grow in those hands once it realizes it is in good hands."

-Idowu Koyenkan

This chapter will cover a crucial topic: the value of managing your company's finances and how to do so with advice and other helpful information. So, hold on tight as we embark on this journey together!

Business finance has to do with managing and raising funds by business establishments. However, the most essential part of your business finance system will be the balance sheet. A balance sheet shows you how much money you owe and how much money you currently have in your account.

If you run a business, you will face several financial challenges. From keeping track of your money to recording sales and expenses, managing your business finances is vital to running a successful business. Some of the most typical forms of business financing include the following:

Cash flow management

A company's cash flow is its monthly balance after paying operating costs. Knowing how much money is coming in, going out and how much is left in the bank helps you predict future financial needs before they occur and, as a result, plan accordingly. The goal of any business owner is to pay as little interest, taxes, and other expenses as possible on their cash inflow.

Capital

Capital refers to the amount of money a business uses for investment purposes, such as buying equipment or expanding operations. It also includes the money needed to pay off loans or other liabilities at maturity.

Inventory management

The cost of goods sold (COGS) consists of three components:

1. **Direct material costs** are associated with the parts or materials used to produce a product or service, including raw materials such as cotton or steel.
2. **Direct labor costs** include wages for workers who make the product or provide the services. This also includes salaries for managers and other staff members who are

directly involved in creating the product or providing services.

3. **Variable manufacturing overhead** is any cost that varies with production volume. This includes departments such as purchasing and accounting, which incur higher fixed costs as volumes increase but do not receive additional compensation for their efforts unless sales increase substantially.

Financing can be short-term (for example, lines of credit) or long-term (for example, loans). A business needs financing when it requires more capital than it has available through cash flows and/or when it wants to purchase equipment or other assets but doesn't have enough money in its current account balance.

A business finance plan is key to managing your business finances. It should be created before you start the day-to-day operations of your business. The program should outline the following:

- The financial goals for the company

- The methods and tools that will be used to achieve those goals

- Where the money will be invested or spent, and how it will be used

- Essential items to continuously keep track of concerning finances

Tips For Managing Your Finances

It would be best if you took the following actions as a small business owner to manage your finances.

1. Pay yourself first.

Trying to condense everything into day-to-day operations can be simple if you manage a small business. After all, having a little extra money can often make a big difference in the expansion of your company. Small business owners must recognize their contribution to the company and pay themselves appropriately. You want to ensure that your personal and business finances are always in order.

2. Invest in expansion.

Budgeting your money while considering growth opportunities is critical. This may help your company grow and move in a sound financial direction. Future planning should always be a priority for business owners.

3. Don't worry about loans.

Understandably, large loans may cause you to start worrying

about the costs of failure. But without the influx of cash that loans provide, expanding your team or buying equipment could be very difficult. Additionally, you can use loan proceeds to improve cash flow, which will help you avoid late payment problems for suppliers and employees.

4. Maintain solid commercial credit.

You might want to buy more commercial real estate as your business expands and more insurance coverage and loans to support these endeavors. However, obtaining approval for all these transactions and acquisitions may be more challenging with lousy business credit.

5. Pay your taxes over time.

Make your quarterly estimated tax payments monthly if you're having trouble saving for them. Tax payments can then be managed similarly to any other monthly operating expense.

6. Develop a sound billing plan.

Every business owner has a client who consistently pays and issues invoices late. Managing small business finances requires you to promptly address these billing problems, allowing you to continue managing cash flow which keeps your business running smoothly.

7. Create sound financial practices.

Establishing internal financial protocols can help to safeguard your company's economic well-being, even if they are as straightforward as designating a regular time for reviewing and updating financial data. In addition, keeping track of your money can help you reduce the risk of fraud.

8. Observe your books.

This is a straightforward but crucial practice. It will give you a better understanding of your company's finances and a window into potential financial crime.

9. Think ahead.

Although there will always be financial issues that need to be resolved, you should always make comprehensive plans for the future. You fall behind the competition if you're not looking five to ten years out regarding money.

Key Takeaways

- If you are running a business, you may likely have many financial challenges, but your ability to keep track of all your expenses and sales helps you to surmount them.

- Even if you're working with a bookkeeper, try to schedule time each day or month to review and monitor your books.

The strategy for marketing and advertising your business to grow will be covered in the following chapter. Let's go!

Chapter 7

Marketing And Promotions

"Stopping advertising to save money is like stopping your watch from saving time."

– Henry Ford

According to a 2017 State of Small Business Report, only three out of ten small businesses invested enough in marketing. This was made evident when 1,100 small business owners were surveyed. This chapter will explore the importance of marketing and promotions and the ways to go about them. Marketing and advertising are crucial because they enable you to deliberately distribute your goods and services to a specific target audience. This makes it easier for you to explain to others how great your company is and how you can assist them.

The most essential function of a promotion is to distinguish a company from its rivals. No business would ever need to conduct promotions if there were zero competition. For clients to continue doing business with you, you must stay one step ahead of your rivals. If another company offers comparable goods or services to yours, you can only convince clients to buy from you if you provide a special deal. Of course, educating the public about promotions through various forms of advertising and marketing is also crucial.

Importance Of Marketing And Promotions

Building and maintaining a reputation

Your company's reputation is based on how it develops and how long it lasts. This is where marketing appears to be a strategy for enhancing a company's brand equity and occurs when customers' expectations are satisfied.

Building a link between customers and the business

Any firm that wants to expand must establish a strong connection with its clients. Marketing is based on consumer behavior, psychographics, and demographics, which helps to understand customers' desires.

Sales growth

Marketing helps increase the possibility of better sales by utilizing various approaches to advertise goods and services. Happy consumers naturally become brand ambassadors for a business.

Remaining relevant

Marketing aids a company in remaining relevant to its

target audience and industry. It supports the pursuit of keeping up positive relationships.

Making educated decisions

Every business' fundamental inquiry centers on the "how" 's and "why" 's of producing goods or providing services. This demonstrates the value of marketing for companies and how it connects them with society.

Marketing Methods

Below are the various marketing tactics that you should be knowledgeable about:

B2C Advertising

Business-to-consumer marketing is referred to as B2C marketing. This describes a business that sells its goods or services to customers and advertises its existence. This is a technique that many business owners use to engage their customers persuasively or effectively. It could be done using television commercials to bring your product to the font. It is mainly done online.

C2B Advertising

This stands for consumer-to-business marketing, which

is the reverse of B2C. The consumer provides the business with goods or services through this marketing.

C2C Marketing

Consumer-to-consumer marketing is referred to as C2C marketing. When using a shared good or service, consumers interact with co-consumers.

Ways To Promote And Market Your Business

Publish a blog and a website

If your business doesn't have a website in today's online environment, you might as well not even exist. Developing a website is always the first step in promoting your company online. Make sure it has your contact information, a description of your product or service, and marketing assets like endorsements, videos showing the product in action, and good reviews. Once you've finished, you can now add a blog.

Use online reviews and media to your advantage

Because almost everyone reads online evaluations and believes them to be reliable, they are one of the most low-cost strategies to market your company. Create a method for collecting and managing online consumer reviews so you can highlight your best ones and address any issues brought up by unhappy customers.

Plan locally

Targeting local clients is one of the best strategies to advertise your company. To get your brand in the local media, you should:

1. Get to know the journalists and newspapers that cover your community and sector.

2. Ask if you can be featured on the websites of companies in the same industry or that sell a product that complements your own.

3. Think about forming a free trade alliance and trading services for publicity or vice versa.

Find the right recommendations

Obtaining referrals for a service business involves skill and careful planning. People are more inclined to purchase your products or use your service if a reliable source recommends it. It might be difficult for new businesses to grow their clientele through recommendations. However, if you take the time to comprehend the psychology of clients who are prepared to recommend you, you'll be able to reach additional clients.

Key Takeaways

- The most essential function of a promotion is to distinguish a company from its rivals.

- Developing a website is always the first step in promoting your company online.

- Marketing and promotion are crucial because they enable you to distribute your goods and services to a specific target deliberately. This makes it easier for you to explain to others how great your company is and how you can assist them.

Depending on your firm's goals, objectives, and priorities, you can utilize a variety of promotional tactics to sell and promote your idea. Without marketing promotions, it would be impossible for preoccupied customers to pay attention to your brand or service.

Conclusion

There are plenty of brilliant ideas; what's lacking is the motivation to put them into action." -Seth Godin

I cannot stress enough how vital these chapters' key points are when venturing to start your own small business. Understanding what you're selling and why someone would want to buy it is one of the most important aspects of a business. When you know who your customers are and what attracts them to your product or service, then and only then are you truly able to develop a successful business.

A business plan is a formal statement of the information you need to launch your business, complete with a marketing plan, operations procedures, and measures for financial success. Business plans are vital for new and existing companies considering expanding or adjusting their operations. Ultimately, the same thing you need to start a business is what you need for self-improvement: knowledge. And if you desire to be innovative and creative within your field, that's something you can only get by being around other innovators and creatives. So, make sure to develop your network, whether formally or informally—and always do it to add more value than you take away.

Entrepreneurship is a learning process, and you'll make mistakes. But that's okay—what's important is that you learn from them and keep moving forward.

SNEAK PEAK: THE PLAYBOOK FOR STARTING A SMALL BUSINESS

THE SMALL BUSINESS WORLD

"A big business starts small." ~ Richard Branson

One of the most competitive and challenging sectors in the economy is the world of small business. The world of small business is made up of a diverse range of organizations and firms, each with its own particular difficulties, possibilities, and rewards. To succeed in a competitive setting, you must be able to identify the factors that contribute to the success of your rivals so that you can employ similar tactics to outperform them.

A great place to begin is by understanding how the small business world works. This chapter will outline everything you need to know about small businesses. Let's start with what strictly a small business is.

What Is a Small Business?

Small companies generally offer services or are retail establishments like grocery stores, pharmacies, tradesmen, and bakeries. Small businesses are privately held companies that need less equipment, labor, and cash than larger companies. These enterprises are ideally suited to run on a micro level to benefit the neighborhood and bring in income for the business owners.

A small business is typically a company that employs fewer than 500 employees. It can be any company, including a sole proprietorship, partnership, or corporation. The term "small business" has been used to describe small enterprises since the 19th century. The Small Business Administration (SBA) defines a small business as one with annual receipts of less than $7 million if located in the United States and less than $10 million outside the United States. There are several different ways businesses can be classified as small or large. One way is by the number of employees they have on staff at any time. Another way is their annual revenue (which may include income and expenses). A third way is by the number of units they produce per year: for example, an industry that has 200 cars per year is considered significant compared to an industry that produces only 100 vehicles per year.

The world of small business is a tough place to get a foothold in. If you want to start a business, you probably have some ideas about what it should do and how it should be structured. You may have even researched the industry that your company will be servicing or selling to, but that's all you have—an idea and a plan. The only way to get started is to take action; take the first step and get going! You need to decide what kind of business you're going to run and how much time and money you're willing to invest in it. Once you've made that decision, it's time to start preparing for the big day—getting ready for your first day as the owner of a small business!

Small businesses are very much vital to the economy and the world. They employ millions of people, support their communities and create jobs.

The characteristics of a small business are many, but the most common are:

What Kind of a Small Business Are You?

The first thing when considering the type of small business that is best for you is what your goals are. Do you just want to make money, or do you want to do something that makes the world a better place? If so, maybe the humanitarian aspect is more important than making money. You could also consider whether or not you have enough knowledge about specific areas that would allow you to run this type of business well. For example, if you're interested in starting an online retail store but don't know how much inventory management costs per month, that's something you can focus on learning before you get started. Let's go over some categories of business.

- **Small Scale Industry**

Small Scale Industry is a small-scale industrial unit that produces less than 100 units of a product. It includes small-scale industries like food processing, pharmaceuticals, chemicals, and pulp and paper, among others.

- **Ancillary Small Industrial Unit**

An Ancillary Small Industrial Unit is a manufacturing unit that provides inputs to other businesses in the production of products. These companies are called ancillary units because they supply raw materials to other businesses for their output. An example of such a company would be a food processor that provides flour to bakeries for bread making.

- **Export Oriented Units**

Export Oriented Units are businesses that export their products overseas. They may not be located in a developed country, but they ship their products to other countries through exports. Examples of these companies are automobile manufacturers who export cars to Asian countries like Japan and China.

- **Minor Scale Service and Businesses**

A Small Service Business is one that provides services to individual customers at the premises where they reside or work rather than having it done at an outside office or facility location. This type of business may include hair salons and dry-cleaning shops.

- **Micro Business Enterprises**

Micro Business Enterprises are small businesses that employ fewer than 100 people. Micro businesses are often referred to as "mom and pop" shops, although the term "micro" may also be used to describe other small businesses such as restaurants, service providers, or manufacturers.

- **Village Industries**

Village Industries are small businesses that operate in rural or semi-rural areas without a large concentration of other small businesses. These businesses may be owned by individuals or families or by nonprofit organizations. They provide goods and services to residents of the community.

- **Cottage Industries**

Cottage Industries are small businesses that produce goods or provide services for local residents. Cottage industries often have a very narrow focus on their products and services, which may mean that they have limited product lines and few employees

Sole Proprietorship

A Sole Proprietorship is a business that is owned and operated by one person. A sole proprietor is responsible for all legal, financial, and operational aspects of his or her business. This is a solid way to start your own business without any legal or financial obligations. However, this also implies that you are personally responsible for everything related to your business.

Partnership

A Partnership is basically an agreement between two or more people with joint ownership interests in an ongoing business enterprise. Partnerships can be formed by anyone who wants to participate in the profits and losses of an ongoing business enterprise. Partnerships have unlimited liability, which means that if one partner breaches the agreement, all partners may be held liable for all the debts and obligations incurred by this breached party.

A Limited Liability

A Limited Liability company is a business setup that offers its members limited personal liability for the debts of the company in exchange for greater management flexibility. A limited liability company is not considered a partnership and does not have the same opportunities for sharing in profits, losses, or other financial gains. However, it can offer many of the same tax benefits as a partnership. The most significant difference between a limited liability company and a partnership is that while partnerships are taxed based on their income and profits, LLCs are taxed based on their earnings only and not their income.

For example, if you owned 100% of an LLC with annual revenue of $1.1 million and expenses of $1 million, your profit would be $100,000 ($1.1 million minus $1 million), but your wages would be subject to payroll taxes at a rate of 15%.

How a Small Business Is Run

A small business is the most common type of company in America. It's also one of the most essential parts of our economy. The way a small business is run can vary, but here are some general guidelines:

- The owner (or owners) is responsible for doing everything that happens at the company. The owner signs all checks, pays all bills, and manages the company's finances.

- There are usually only a few employees at a small company—usually one or two. They're responsible for carrying out their duties on a daily basis so that customers receive good service while they're in-store or online and making sure that things run smoothly behind the scenes so that customers don't notice any problems during their visits or online purchases.

- The owner also hires people to help with various tasks like marketing and accounting, as well as hiring temporary workers when needed during peak seasons or busy times of the year.

- Small businesses typically have an office space where members of staff meet regularly to discuss how to move things forward and how it will be accomplished. They may also have a conference room for meetings with clients, vendors, or other stakeholders about projects or new ideas for expansion. A successful small business is the result of a number of factors, but the most important is the owner's ability to manage his or her time and resources effectively. Here are some tips to help you do just that.

Prioritize tasks by importance

Once you have a list of tasks, rank them from most important (1) to least significant (5). Then create sub-tasks within each primary task based on how much time it requires and how critical it is to get things done right now rather than later.

Be Dedicated

Successful businesses are run with a common purpose and common goals in mind. They're also run by people who are passionate about their product or service and want to be successful at what they do. Business owners must be willing to sacrifice time with their family and friends for the sake of their business.

Make a plan

A good plan will help you prioritize tasks, track progress, and stay on track toward achieving your goals for your business. Start by creating a work schedule for yourself each week so you know what times of day you'll be working on different projects each day. This can help keep your schedule organized and give you room for flexibility if necessary (e.g., emergencies).

Small Business Impact on the World

Small businesses are majorly a part of the world economy, and their impact on the world is profound. The World Bank estimates that over 90% of the world's small businesses are locally owned, but they also account for more than 90% of all private-sector employment (World Bank). Since small businesses are so prevalent in every country around the globe, they have a tremendous impact on the global economy.

Small business owners represent an important source of new jobs in developing countries. Small businesses create jobs for people who might not otherwise have work, especially if they live far from an industrial area. They also provide higher-paying jobs to those unemployed or underemployed.

Small businesses also play quite an important role in creating wealth for countries and individuals within those countries. For example, over 20 million small businesses in India generate more than $1 trillion annually (World Bank). This money goes into local economies, which grows the local economy and helps increase job opportunities for everyone living there, including those who do not own a business themselves but still use its services.

Foolish Assumptions in Running a Business

There are plenty of assumptions you can make about running a business. But there are also some foolish assumptions that you should avoid at all costs. Here are two common assumptions that I see all the time.

1. You have to be an expert in everything.

2. You have to be able to work 24/7.

I'll start by dispelling the first one: You don't need to be an expert in everything related to running your business. Most small businesses don't have the resources or expertise to do that. So if you're starting, it's probably better for your sanity and long-term success if you avoid making bad decisions because of misinformation or fear of failure when you're still learning the ropes of running your own business.

Now let's talk about the second one: You don't have to work every day (unless you want to). Anyone who tells you they do is most likely either lying or exaggerating. Some people may need more structure than others, but if they're not enjoying their job, then they're doing something wrong

Small Business vs. Large Business

As I have stated in this book, Small Business is a business with fewer than 500 employees, while a Large Business is a business with 500 or more employees. Small businesses can be either privately owned or publicly held. In contrast, large businesses are usually publicly traded. They often provide value to their owners through dividends or services or products that are essential to the company's overall function.

In general, small businesses tend to be family-owned and operated. In addition to providing employment opportunities for individuals in the community, small businesses provide an opportunity for anyone to kickstart their own business. They become self-employed, or they can choose to work for someone else (either within their own family or outside) who owns a small business.

Large businesses may also include corporations that have grown from smaller companies over time. For example, a corporation may have been founded as a partnership between two friends but has grown into a multinational corporation with thousands of employees worldwide. Let's look at some of the other major differences between a large and small business.

- **Size**

One major difference between a large and small company is the size. Large companies have more resources and employees than small ones, which means they can do things impossible for a small company to do without outside help. For example, large companies can afford to hire a team of lawyers and accountants. In contrast, small businesses often have no choice but to use less experienced professionals who may not be as skilled or knowledgeable.

- **Leadership**

Small businesses tend to be run by a single person or family, while large companies often have several owners or managers. This can make it difficult for large companies to work together effectively because no one is responsible for making decisions that affect the entire company. Smaller businesses tend to have more clearly defined leadership structures so that everyone knows who is accountable for what actions in their area of responsibility.

- **Marketing**

When it comes to marketing efforts, large companies usually have more resources than smaller ones because they can afford better advertising campaigns and more sophisticated marketing strategies than smaller businesses can manage on their own budgets alone.

Takeaway

- The key difference between big and small businesses is their size. Big businesses have more employees, meaning they have more overhead costs than smaller businesses.

- A small business is typically a company that employs fewer than 500 employees. It can be any company, including a sole proprietorship, partnership, or corporation.

- Small business owners represent an important source of new jobs in developing countries. Small businesses create jobs for people who might not otherwise have work, especially if they live far from an industrial area.

- The best way to start a small business is to find something you are passionate about and then build it. Then you can learn the skills and knowledge needed to build your product or service, starting with the functionality and adding more features as you go along.

You have probably heard the term "successful business owners" before, but what does it even mean? What makes a successful business owner?

You will find out all this and much more so check out: The Playbook to Starting a Small Business Owners. In it I cover essential topics and detail how to help you start your small business.

Are you ready? Purchase it today!

Resources

Adams (2022), "Business plan" from https://www.investopedia.com/terms/b/business-plan.asp

Brain Sutter (2020) "5 Surprising Facts About Small Business Marketing" Retrieved from 5 Surprising Facts About Small Business Marketing - AllBusiness.com

Insight (2017) "BUSINESS OWNERS: WHAT IS YOUR VALUE PROPOSITION?" retrieved from https://insquired.com/business-owners-what-is-your-value-proposition-plus-examples/#:~:text=A%20value%20proposition%20is%20what,pick%20you%20over%20your%20competition.

Jennifer (2019) "The art of selling as a business owner" retrieved from https://www.forbes.com/sites/theyec/2019/01/09/the-art-of-selling-as-a-business-owner/?sh=76b80e3976b4

Jonathan (2017) "The Entrepreneur's Guide to Building a Successful Business" retrieved from https://efmdglobal.org/wp-content/uploads/The-Entrepreneurs-Guide-to-Building-a-Successful-Business-2017.pdf

Joseph (2021) "Founders! Are you listening: when it into all good to not shy to ask for help?" retrieved from https://dutchuncles.in/aspire/founders-are-you-listening-when-it-is-not-all-good-do-not-shy-to-ask-for-help/

Marcus Taylor (2020) "Marketing Expert" Retrieved from 32

Inspiring Quotes From Marketing Experts (ventureharbour.com)

Matt (2022) "10 tips for managing small Business Finances" retrieved from https://www.businessnewsdaily.com/5954-smb-finance-management-tips.html

Peep (2019) "How to Create a Unique Value Proposition (with Examples)" retrieved from https://cxl.com/blog/value-proposition-examples-how-to-create

Peter Daisyme (2022)" 7 characteristics of a successful entrepreneur "Retrieved from https://www.entrepreneur.com/article/285466#:~:text=Mindset%20%2D%2D%20a%20strong%20and,attitudes%20and%20feelings%20about%20ourselves.

Susan (2019) "How to make money in Business" retrieved from https://www.thebalancesmb.com/business-money-makers-2948297